THUNDERSTORMS

A TRUE BOOK

by

**Paul P. and
Diane M. Sipiera**

Children's Press®

A Division of Grolier Publishing

New York London Hong Kong Sydney
Danbury, Connecticut

Reading Consultant
Linda Cornwell
Learning Resource Consultant
Indiana Department
of Education

Authors' Dedication
To our little thunderstorm,
Caroline Antarctica Sipiera

A thunderstorm over
St. Paul, Minnesota

Visit Children's Press® on the Internet at:
http://publishing.grolier.com

Library of Congress Cataloging-in-Publication Data

Sipiera, Paul P.
    Thunderstorms / by Paul P. and Diane M. Sipiera.
        p.   cm. — (A true book)
    Includes bibliographical references and index.
    Summary: Introduces thunderstorms by explaining the weather condi-
tions which cause them and describing the damage which severe storms
can cause.
    ISBN: 0-516-20680-X (lib.bdg.)   0-516-26442-7(pbk.)
    1. Thunderstorms—Juvenile literature. [1. Thunderstorms.] I. Sipiera,
Diane M.   II. Title.   III. Series.
QC968.2.S56   1998
551.55`4—dc21   97-37151
                                                                          CIP
                                                                          AC

Contents

Lightning flashes during a thunderstorm over the Grand Canyon.

The Power of Nature

One of nature's most powerful creations is a thunderstorm. One of the best places in the United States to watch a thunderstorm is the Grand Canyon, in Arizona. From the top of the canyon, you can see for miles. Sometimes, especially during the summer, big thunderstorms take place there. It may not be easy to see the flashes of lightning because they happen so fast. However, you can easily hear the thunder boom as it echoes through the canyon.

Another exciting place to watch thunderstorms is the Great Plains area of the United States. There, you can see dark clouds move in from far away. Bright flashes of lightning can take you by surprise. The way the ground seems to shake as

The high walls of the Grand Canyon (left) make thunder echo over long distances. A thunderstorm rolls in over the Great Plains (above).

thunder rolls by can be a little scary. But many thunderstorms last for only a short time.

Changing Weather

Earth experiences many different kinds of weather. Weather is the condition of the outside air at a certain time or place. Weather can be described as hot or cold, wet or dry, calm or windy, and clear or cloudy.

Earth is covered with an atmosphere (AT-muhss-fir). It

A coat, scarf, hat, and mittens mean cold weather (top). Kite-flying is a fun activity in windy weather (middle). A cloudless sky is a sign of clear weather (bottom).

keeps the temperature from getting too hot or too cold. Earth's atmosphere is always moving. Warm, moist air rises from Earth's equator (i-KWAY-tur). This warm air moves in a circular pattern toward the North and South Poles. The air at the poles is cool and dry. The warm, moist air mixes with the cool, dry air. This mixture, as well as Earth's rotation, creates weather.

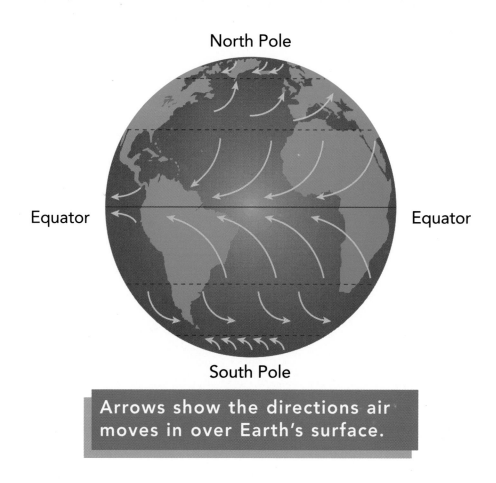

North Pole

Equator

Equator

South Pole

Arrows show the directions air moves in over Earth's surface.

Weather on Earth is usually calm. However, weather can change. When weather changes, thunderstorms can form. Some people fear

Clouds build up near a windmill in Wyoming. This is a sign that the weather is changing.

approaching thunderstorms. This is because thunderstorms can produce both hurricanes and tornadoes.

Understanding Thunderstorms

There are certain weather factors needed to make thunderstorms. First, the air should be warm and moist. Second, a cold front must be present. A cold front is the edge of a huge mass of cold air that pushes warm air out of the way. The cold front can create a strong,

This mass of clouds is a cold front moving over Lake Michigan.

upward movement of air. This upward movement is called an updraft. These two factors can create two kinds of thunderstorms: air-mass thunderstorms or severe thunderstorms.

Air-mass thunderstorms usually form over large bodies of warm water. As the air mass moves over the land, it is heated. As the air mass gets warmer, it can produce storms over a large area. These storms usually occur in the middle of the day. This is when the the ground temperature is hottest. These storms will produce lightning, thunder, and heavy rain. Air-mass thunderstorms are more

Lightning can move from cloud to cloud, from cloud to ground, or from ground to cloud.

common in mountainous areas than over flat land.

Severe thunderstorms usually develop along, or in front of, an approaching cold front.

These giant storms can bring strong winds, hail, tornadoes, heavy rain, and lightning. A severe thunderstorm usually covers a large area.

Compared to the size of a quarter, these hail stones are quite large.

Severe thunderstorms most often occur during the spring and early summer. This is the right time for warm, moist air from the equator to meet cool, dry polar air. There is a big temperature difference

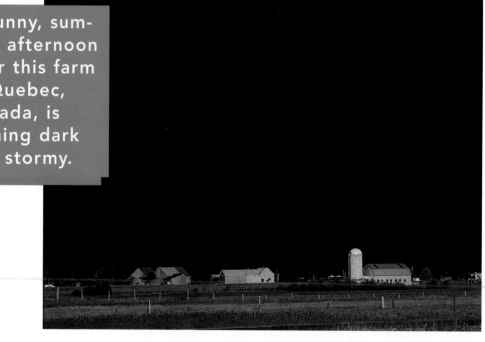

A sunny, summer afternoon over this farm in Quebec, Canada, is turning dark and stormy.

Storm clouds build over Denver, Colorado.

between the two air masses. The cool air moves the warm air out of the way in a rapid, upward manner. The air pressure, or the weight of the air,

The study of approaching storms has helped scientists learn more about what causes them.

also changes. This forms an air current. Updrafts and clouds then form. All of these different factors must happen at the same time to cause a severe thunderstorm.

Thunder and Lightning

For hundreds of years, people have wondered about thunder and lightning. Long ago, people feared thunder and lightning. Today, scientists have a better understanding of what causes them.

Lightning occurs when electricity (i-lek-TRISS-uh-tee), or

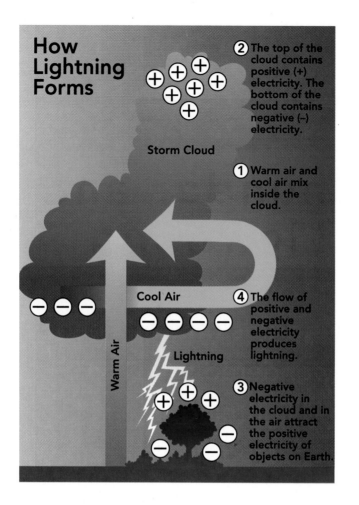

How Lightning Forms

② The top of the cloud contains positive (+) electricity. The bottom of the cloud contains negative (–) electricity.

Storm Cloud

① Warm air and cool air mix inside the cloud.

Cool Air

④ The flow of positive and negative electricity produces lightning.

Warm Air

Lightning

③ Negative electricity in the cloud and in the air attract the positive electricity of objects on Earth.

energy, builds up inside large, dark storm clouds. There are two kinds of electricity: positive and negative. The bottom of the storm cloud holds negative electricity. The top of the storm cloud holds positive electricity. Negative electricity builds up at the bottom of the cloud. Eventually, the negative electricity leaks out of the cloud into the air. Objects on Earth, such as trees, also have positive and negative electricity. The negative electricity in the cloud and in the air is attracted to the positive electricity of objects on Earth. This flow of positive and negative electricity produces lightning.

Ancient Beliefs

In ancient, or long ago, times, people in Greece believed that lightning belonged to the god, Zeus. Zeus was believed to be the king of the gods. Any place where Zeus had thrown lightning was considered very holy. Three one-eyed giants, called Cyclopes, made thunderbolts that Zeus could throw at Earth.

Ancient Greeks believed Zeus controlled lightning.

For an instant, the sky brightens from a lightning flash.

Lightning has two parts: the flash and the strokes. The flash usually lasts for less than a second. It is over before you can blink your eyes. The flash can be seen in the sky as a bright

streak of light. Each flash is really made up of three or four smaller parts. These parts are called the strokes. One part of the stroke leads downward. It is quickly followed by a bright return stroke.

26

Lightning can be danger-
ous. Sometimes, people are
struck by lightning. Each year,
about one hundred people
are killed by lightning.

Lightning strikes can also
cause forest fires. Many scientists believe that fires started

Lightning can
strike trees or
brush, and cause
a forest fire.

by lightning can be good for the forests. Some forest fires "clean" the forest to make room for new plants and trees to grow. But if these fires get out of control, they can threaten lives and property.

Lightning and thunder happen at the same time. Lightning travels so fast that the flash is over in an instant. Thunder travels much slower than lightning. It takes about five seconds for thunder to travel 1 mile (2 kilometers). If

From a safe place, watch for lightning. Count the seconds until you hear thunder. How far away are you from the lightning?

you hear thunder ten seconds after you see lightning, you are about 2 miles (3 km) from the lightning flash. Sometimes people see lightning, but they don't hear thunder. This lightning is called heat lightning.

29

Tornadoes

Severe thunderstorms can result in tornadoes. The funnel shape of a tornado may already be familiar to you. A tornado is really a rotating column of air that comes down from storm clouds. Air near the ground will rush up into the tornado. The winds inside

The funnel shape of a tornado makes it easy to spot.

a tornado can travel up to 300 miles (480 km) per hour.

Tornadoes can form when severe thunderstorms bring high winds, heavy rain, and

Most of this Arkansas town was destroyed by a March 1997 tornado.

large hail. Meteorologists (scientists who study the weather) use special equipment to watch for tornadoes. If a severe thunderstorm is spotted, meteorologists warn people to look out for funnel-shaped clouds. If a funnel is spotted, a tornado is likely. When a tornado appears, people are told to stay in a safe place until the danger passes.

A meteorologist studies a radar screen to observe developing weather.

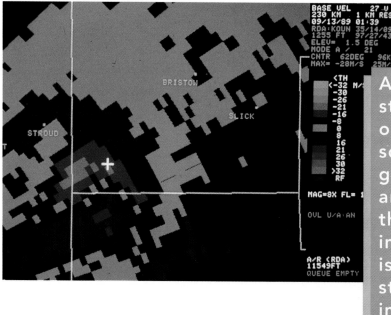

A developing storm is shown on a computer screen. The green and red areas mean that the wind speed inside the storm is very high. This storm may turn into a tornado.

Each year, there are about 770 tornadoes in the United States. Tornadoes can occur during any month of the year. But most tornadoes occur between the months of April and June. The fewest tornadoes occur during the months of December and January. Some areas of the United States experience more tornadoes than other areas. Tornadoes are so common in the Great Plains that the area has been called Tornado Alley.

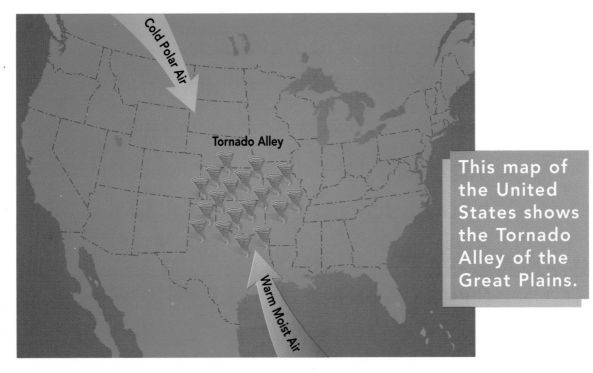

This map of the United States shows the Tornado Alley of the Great Plains.

A tornado's funnel can be long and thin. It can also be wide and stubby. Most tornadoes are black in color. This is the result of soil and debris that they pick up from the ground.

People who have seen tornadoes say that they sound like the noise made by a passing train. The damage done by a tornado can also be unusual. A tornado may destroy all the houses on one side of a street,

This huge, black tornado (above) swept through Cantrall, Illinois, in 1995. Many of the homes at the bottom of this picture (right) were destroyed by a tornado. The homes at the top of the picture were not damaged.

while the houses on the other side of the street are not damaged at all.

Dangerous Thunderstorms

Severe thunderstorms can also cause serious damage. Many thunderstorms bring strong winds. These winds can damage crops. They can also knock down trees and power lines. In addition, heavy rains often cause flash floods. (Flash floods occur when large

Trees and power lines in this Connecticut town were brought down during a serious thunderstorm.

amounts of water flow quickly through an area.) If large hail stones fall, they, too, can destroy farm crops. Hail can also damage automobiles by denting them. The windows of

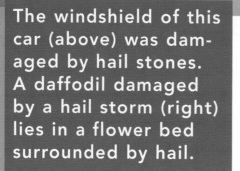

The windshield of this car (above) was damaged by hail stones. A daffodil damaged by a hail storm (right) lies in a flower bed surrounded by hail.

cars and houses are sometimes broken by hail. People have been hurt by large hail stones. Some small animals have been killed by them.

Airplanes and Thunderstorms

Most jet planes are hit by lightning about once a year.

Thunderstorms can be especially dangerous for the pilots of airplanes. Flying through a thunderstorm can cause an airplane to bounce around. Sometimes, airplanes are struck by lightning. When this happens, there is usually no damage to the plane or passengers. Airplanes are covered by a metal "skin." The lightning travels through the skin, and then moves toward the ground.

This plane is carrying researchers directly into a thunderstorm so they can study it.

As you have read, Earth has active weather. The weather can be quite varied and unusual. It results in thunderstorms, lightning, tornadoes, and more. Other planets, such as Jupiter, Saturn, Uranus, and Neptune may also experience

Thunderstorms may take place on the planet, Saturn.

A thunderstorm over Cheyenne, Wyoming

thunderstorms. (Lightning flashes on Jupiter can be the size of the United States!) Venus may experience thunderstorms too. But you don't have to be on other planets to appreciate how amazing thunderstorms can be.

To Find Out More

Here are some additional resources to help you learn more about thunderstorms, tornadoes, lightning, and more:

 **Books**

Byars, Betsy. **Tornado.** HarperCollins Children's Books, 1996.

Davis, Kay and Wendy Oldsfield. **Weather.** Raintree Steck-Vaughn, 1991.

Kramer, Stephen. **Lightning.** Lerner, 1993.

Palmer, Joy. **Rain.** Raintree Steck-Vaughn, 1992.

Sipiera, Paul P. and Diane M. Sipiera. **Wildfires.** Children's Press, 1998.

Tripp, Nathaniel. **Thunderstorm!** Dial Books for Young Readers, 1994

Organizations and Online Sites

National Center for Atmospheric Research (NCAR)

P. O. Box 3000
Boulder, CO 80307
http://www.ncar.edu

Conducts research into how changes in Earth's atmosphere affect the weather in different seasons. Includes links to other sites.

National Weather Service

http://www.yahoo.com/ government/National_ Weather_Service/

Find out what kind of weather you can expect with each new season, as well as the kinds of storms that can occur. You can also watch a severe storm as it develops.

The Weather Channel

http://www.weather.com/ twc/

See how the weather changes from season to season. There's also a glossary of weather words, and links to other sites.

Thunderstorms and Lightning

http://www.hgea.org/E911/ thunder.htm

Here you'll discover how many thunderstorms are taking place on Earth at any given moment. You'll also find lightning safety rules, and places you can write to for more facts and statistics.

Important Words

canyon deep, narrow river valley with steep sides

debris remains of things that have been broken or destroyed

equator imaginary line around the middle of Earth

hail balls of ice that can fall during a thunderstorm

hurricane tropical storm with wind speeds of more than 70 miles (115 km) per hour

nature everything in the world not made by people, such as plants, animals, and the weather

Index

Meet the Authors

Paul and Diane Sipiera share the same interest in science and nature. Paul is a college professor in Palatine, Illinois. Diane is the director of education for the Planetary Studies Foundation of Algonquin, Illinois. Together with their daughters Andrea, Paula, and Carrie Ann, the Sipieras enjoy their small farm in Galena, Illinois.

COMMUNITY
CORPORATION